KEIKO MAEDA IN KYOTO
photos by ANDERS EDSTRÖM

THE SPRING PRESS

New York, New York

SP#29 published in association with COSMIC WONDER
Essay by Cameron Allan McKean

IN GLASS

Cameron Allan McKean

In 1962, a team of Japanese archaeologists traveled to Nara Prefecture, near Kyoto, to begin excavating a constellation of burial mounds that would become known as the "Niizawa Senzuka Kofun Cluster." The 590 tumuli at this site — now surrounded by small farms and narrow roads — contain thousands of ancient objects, buried alongside people who lived in this area between the third and seventh centuries.

The excavations would take years. Each tomb was numbered and the objects buried inside were named and archived. In 1963, work began on Tumulus No. 126, a burial mound like many others in the cluster — relatively large (16 m by 22 m) and containing a cache of funerary objects arrayed around a wooden coffin made from a single tree.

"Long thin strip-shaped object," "Fragments of iron swords," "Gold square plate" and "Mirror without decorative pattern" were the names given to some of the first items the archaeologists found around the coffin. Opening its lid they found a body covered in pieces of jewellery that would later be catalogued as: "Gold bracelet," "Gold hair ornaments," "Gold rings," "Silver bracelet," "Silver ring," "Fragments of silver ring" and "Gilt bronze buckle for obi belt." There were also glass

objects scattered around the deceased, including "Glass beads with striped pattern," "Comma-shaped jadeite," "Comma-shaped jewel," "Globular-shaped glass beads," and "Globular shaped glass bead containing gold leaf." These were not rare or especially unusual objects.

And then there is "Glass bowl."

"Glass bowl placed on top of glass dish was retrieved from the right side of the head of the deceased," says the record of The National Institutes for Cultural Heritage. "Made from alkali glass, the glass bowl has a light yellow green color with a thickness of 1.5 mm and is extremely light in weight. The base of the bowl has two layers of circular motifs inscribed and five layers of motifs around its waist." These inscriptions are illegible.

There was nothing else like these pieces of glassware in the entire tumulus cluster, or almost anywhere else in 5th-century Japan. Although the blue glass dish it was placed upon has received more attention in the years since it was discovered (perhaps because of its brilliant color and the fact that it was made in the Roman Empire), it's the bowl I'm more interested in.

The smell of wet soil fills the air — the smell of an open quarry after a storm. It's 1963, the first day of excavations on Tumulus No. 126. We push past researchers and workers wearing sweat-stained cotton shirts to get closer to the archaeologists nearest to the coffin. The lid is off and they're leaning over its walls to pick up the bowl. It's the first time the bowl has been held in over 1,000 years. Lifted out carefully, sunlight begins to pass through it. The archaeologist, now holding the bowl up, sees the far end of the tumulus through its surface, sees the outline of the coffin, sees the details of her own fingers holding it, and then she looks into the glass itself.

It's not perfectly transparent, but about as close as humanity had come to perfect clarity at the start of the first millennium. Holding it up to the light, tiny frozen plumes of impurities — bits of silica, lime or plant ash that did not melt together — reveal themselves. It's believed the bowl was made in the Sasanid Persian Empire around two centuries before being buried in Tumulus No. 126 and typical of Sasanian glass, it's uncolored and without excessive decoration.

Looking into the bowl, the archaeologist imagines the first time the person in the coffin also held it, what they would have thought as they raised it to the light, how they would have seen their own reflection in its surface, how they would have looked into the glass and imagined it being created centuries before. Although much of it is transparent, the history, usage and creation of the bowl remains largely obscured.

At the far end of this cave of unknowns is a glass maker in Persia, blowing molten liquid into the shape of a bowl. Once the object has cooled, they hold it up, look inside it, and see not just their own reflection but envision the bowl's first owner, who will also hold it and look inside it. Each successive owner — purchasing or trading the bowl as it travels hand-to-hand along the Silk Road — is picturing the past and future of the object while they look into its glassy surface. And over days, over decades, a nascent desire for transparency begins to take shape. If this bowl could be created, what else is possible? The transparent world begins to crystallize.

The markings of "Glass bowl," now completely illegible, fade as it is handled and touched over the years. But it receives new inscriptions as it's carried, each time it is scratched, dropped, hit, stolen, lost and rediscovered, forgotten and remembered. And as these incidental marks accumulate in layers, "Glass bowl" reciprocates, leaving inscriptions on those who own it.

One night, a century after it is made, an owner traveling with it falls asleep. They dream of the bowl. Its glassy reflections are muted in the light of dawn as it sits on a rocky peak. And as the sun rises, so does the bowl; it floats up, bobbing in the cold air. With each lick of the wind it becomes more like liquid, slowly taking on new forms. First it's shaped into a taurus-like doughnut, then a greebled cube, and then a dense, compressed, multicoloured city of cavernous light-filled glass spaces, all visible as the sunlight passes through surface after surface with perfect openness and clarity.

"The most ineffable, most elementary, most flexible and most changeable of materials, richest in meaning and inspiration, fusing with the world like no other. This least fixed of materials transforms itself with every change of atmosphere. It is infinitely rich in relations, mirroring what is above, below, and what is below, above. It is animated, full of spirit and alive," wrote architectural critic Adolf Behne in the October 1915 edition of the journal "Kunstgewerbeblatt."

The living transparency has been called by many names. The etymology of the word glass reveals that its earliest forms — *glas, gler, glæs, glasam, glodus, gladuku, glar, ghel* — did not refer to transparency but instead to smoothness, to a shining quality, or even to colors such as green, blue and grey. Natural glass, such as volcanic obsidian or the preternaturally green glass created by meteors crashing into the Earth's surface, is just as opaque. Early glass was a material full of the desire for transparency but incapable of achieving it. When our ancestors looked into it, they saw plumes of coloured minerals and half-recognizable reflections.

But at some point the possibility of total transparency emerged, a clarity found in some early windows made in the Roman Empire and also in examples of glassware from the Sasanian Empire. A clarity which would be perfected with the mass production of inexpensive sheet glass during the mid-19th century.

After its journey across the Silk Road, the bowl arrives in Japan. It's a precious, rare object, far from home. Tribespeople during Japan's Kofun Period lay it in the tumulus that will one day be called "No. 126" as baggage for the dead person inside to take into the afterlife.

Then that first archaeologist is seeing it in 1963, first in the coffin, then while holding it up as they see the bowl being seen across time. Then it's resting on a cataloging table and is placed in storage and, finally, in a Tokyo museum, behind more glass, which is where I am seeing it now.

The fragile, clear bowl, marked by cracks and illegible inscriptions, rises up into the air.

I am now sitting behind a piece of sheet glass in a city in Japan. Through it, I can see skyscrapers in the distance, many of which are built with glass facades. The sun is setting and the buildings are reflecting the colored afternoon light back across the city.

"Buildings like crystal / Walls of translucent glass / Sheer glass blocks sheathing a steel grill / No gothic branch: no Acanthus leaf: no recollection of the plant world / A mineral kingdom." That was how architectural illustrator Hugh Ferriss visualized the built environment of the future his 1929 book "The Metropolis of Tomorrow." Others looked out at a similar view. The same year, Buckminster Fuller and Isamu Noguchi discussed the possibility of a world without shadows — a totally reflective, utopian environment of glasslike surfaces. "The new glass milieu will transform humanity utterly. And now it remains only to be wished that the new glass-culture will not encounter too many enemies," wrote Walter Benjamin in his essay "Experience and Poverty" in 1933 about his desire for a transparent world without "traces."

The tiny glass seed planted in the first millennium had grown into the possibility of a utopian world without shadows by the 1920s and '30s.

I'm looking out at a very strange approximation of that world.

Focusing my eyes closer, I try to stop looking through the glass in front of me and to instead see into it, to see inside the substance creating this mineral, traceless milieu.

What I see is a large pane of ubiquitous, clear sheet glass. I see the same homogenous transparency that is everywhere in the built environment. This window is no different to the window across the street, no different to the window on the bus passing by, to the piece of glass covering the digital display I am viewing these words on, no different to a glass heart, or a light-filled transparent city; a homogenous substance without traces.

There is no evidence of how the sheet glass in front of me was made. There is no evidence of its history or even its own materiality, no impurities, no traces of anything, no matter how intently I stare. In fact, I start to wonder if it is possible to look inside transparent modern glass at all. The only thing that can be seen as you stare inside it, slowly allowing your eyes to focus, is a reflection of your own face; a light-faded, spectral, uncanny resemblance; a likeness hovering in the glass over a busy street, penetrated by pedestrians, traffic, competing shadows and reflections.

KEIKO MAEDA IN KYOTO photos by ANDERS EDSTRÖM

Published by The Spring Press in association with Cosmic Wonder
SP#29 was printed in an edition of five hundred copies
Photographs commissioned by Cosmic Wonder 2011—2012
Design *Jeff Burch.* Special thanks to *Stefan Ohlsson* and *Stephen Sprott*
Copyright © 2015 Cosmic Wonder, Anders Edström and The Spring Press
ISBN: 978-0-9909377-0-8